PRAISE

I Thought There Would Be More Wolves offers a bold voice, fierce and vulnerable. I admire that while it engages pain it does not stay in that space of hurt but pushes beyond to what's next.

    —Elizabeth Bradfield, author of *Toward Antarctica*

Sara Ryan's debut is full of childhood, last chances, taxonomies of solitude, and the ways the wolves in all of us can be groomed by both nature and nurture. Each of the extinctions of self and world are bloody but rife with a courageous loneliness and keen questions. In this book the dead are searched, known, and fully articulated—the birds, the moose, the ghosts. Even if everything is "too final for its own good," Ryan can make it live again in language. She renders our survival red, and bone, and animal in all our gorgeous and solitary skins.

    —Traci Brimhall, author of *Come the Slumberless to the Land of Nod*

Sara Ryan's exquisitely wrought *I Thought There Would Be More Wolves* carries the charm, irony and frightening ferocity of unexpurgated fairy tales, the original stories spoken in the dusk, drawing up both bone and fur, feather, and blood. This is a collection that admits transmutation. The central question being can we bear what we become any more than what we are? A girl who swallows her soft teeth grows into a woman with harder, sharper teeth. Baring them at will or as necessary or suddenly startling us. These poems speak from "the dirt sweet sweat of the mouth." Where are the wolves? Ryan knows they reside inside us alongside birds, deer, even the humble butterfly. Teeth, flesh, chrysalis, we are the bestiary in the mirror standing before ourselves in fear and awe. Read this poignant and unflinching book to be welcomed with a "hood of antlers" in the shadows of a room. Reread it to find the antlers are yours.

    —Vievee Francis, author of *Forest Primeval*

In *I Thought There Would Be More Wolves*, Sara Ryan writes with ferocious energy about all the ways "a girl learns how to best survive" in a violent and lonely world, a world of hunters and butchers who treat girls like creatures to be caged, controlled, and consumed. She explores the desire to become the wolf instead of the prey animal, the thing with teeth and claws—a survivor of the forest—and the poems here embrace that wild spirit, are full of striking imagery, rich language, and emotional urgency. Visceral and raw, tender and lyrical, this is a fierce and feral debut.

—Sara Eliza Johnson, author of *Bone Map*

In these shape-shifting poems, Sara Ryan moves back and forth between the speaker who is made of fragile flesh and the one who wants to tear that flesh from the bone. "I was never a wolf, but a girl," she writes, though her poems fearlessly plunge their teeth into whatever they happen upon, including pressing questions of identity and agency: What does it mean to be both predator and prey? To run from memory and hunt it down at the same time? To claim a body while writing an elegy to it? As Ryan says, "when I promised my mother I wouldn't dig up bones / for a living, I only meant . . . the bones / that didn't belong to me." Here is a book that doesn't flinch from the hard work of chewing on not only the bones but also the heart."

—Keetje Kuipers, author of *All Its Charms*

I Thought There Would Be More Wolves

I THOUGHT THERE WOULD BE MORE WOLVES

poems

SARA RYAN

UNIVERSITY OF ALASKA PRESS

FAIRBANKS

Text © 2021
University of Alaska Press

Published by
University of Alaska Press
P.O. Box 756240
Fairbanks, AK 99775-6240

Cover and interior design by UA Press.

Cover artwork by Hanna Lee Joshi. The Wilds I. *hannaleejoshi.com*

Library of Congress Cataloging-in-Publication Data

Names: Ryan, Sara, 1992- author.
Title: I Thought There Would Be More Wolves / by Sara Ryan.
Description: Fairbanks, AK : University of Alaska Press, [2021]
Identifiers: LCCN 2020030576 (print) | LCCN 2020030577 (ebook) | ISBN
    9781602234499 (paperback) | ISBN 9781602234505 (ebook)
Subjects: LCGFT: Poetry.
Classification: LCC PS3618.Y3436 I33 2021 (print) | LCC PS3618.Y3436
    (ebook) | DDC 811/.6—dc23
LC record available at https://lccn.loc.gov/2020030576
LC ebook record available at https://lccn.loc.gov/2020030577

For my family,
for the wolves,
for the not-yet-extinct among us

All stories are about wolves. All worth repeating, that is…
There's escaping from the wolves, fighting the wolves,
capturing the wolves, taming the wolves. Being thrown to
the wolves or throwing others to the wolves so the wolves
will eat them instead of you. Running with the wolf pack.
Turning into a wolf. Best of all, turning into the head wolf.
No other decent stories exist.

—Margaret Atwood

CONTENTS

Self-Portrait as Mammal

I have been lost for some time now. the hunt
    has been long and cold. and maybe

it has all been for nothing.   listen:
    my cat and I sleep back to back like two

mirrored moons. this is how I learned
    my body's soft groan. its clumsy

bones growing heavier each night. this is when
    fur tangles and emerges from my mouth

like a wolf. it is something familiar—I call it
    beast and it grows teeth.   somehow,

the only thing I fear is the dull knock of my heart.
    its dangerous call into the wild.   to quench

its cry, I undress and redress and undress again
    in front of the window like the whole world

can see me. I glow like lamplight. like some
    tropical and unnamed creature. feathered

and clawed. fowl or forked tongue.　　　　　　what

　　　　would it take? to be an assassin of my body's

claim to blood and pain.　　　　　　　　I wish I could be

　　　　as flashy as the waterfall. as Niagara's roar.

it spills and does not stop. even when engineers

　　　　divert the water and it becomes a drizzle. even

when a bird flies into the rush. even when

　　　　I shiver in the mist. lean into the spray.

I

… The wolf, broken and bleeding—
That was me.
                    —*Cynthia Cruz*

Wolf Question

what do you call a lost wolf?
she moves like water and shadows. she combs

the snow for deer mice, sweet bushes dense
with blueberries. she has tremendous stamina.

forty-two strong and ripping teeth.
she separates from the pack.

> *

> what do you call a lost girl?
> she moves like a flurry of starlings,

> a dark and twisting shape. she carves
> out a hole in the earth and counts

> the days that crawl by. she thinks,
> sometimes, that it is easier to be alone.

I Thought There Would Be More Wolves

here. at the dumb stroke of midnight. in the glass dome of roses.
the woods at the end of the lake. I was taught where to wait
patiently. to fold my hands on my lap like two sorry doves. to tie
my shoes in knots too tight to unravel. it's incredible how the oceans
meet and trade salinity. how carbonation stings our throats but we keep
drinking. I was never a wolf, but a girl with a red-brick house. a girl with
a bicycle made of puzzle pieces. I wasn't a deer. I wasn't a lamb. all my wars
with the concrete were over. I'm driving alone to everywhere I am going.
I can't strip my skin away. my fur. my wolf teeth. yellow and dull.

Your Daughter Is a Liar

she never repainted the bedroom. she said the steak was well-seasoned. she
brushed out the braids you made and said it was the rain.

what a waste to have collected her trophies. what a waste to have fed
the lizard translucent crickets until it died. what a waste to have groomed

the horses until they gleamed. on the bathroom floor, her nose bleeds
until it is dark and dried. until her eyes are smooth grey stones. when

does she finish feeling like a fortune. when does she learn to crack
the eggs into the bowl without shell. when does she stop walking by

the church like a silly angel in white. and now, she has managed to sleep
without forgetting to open the window. without swallowing the spiders

in her mouth. don't worry, this is not how she goes. not easy, not in
the night. not without spilling her name like milk.

Nesting Material

when I was a girl from Michigan,
my father's feelings were hurt. every

man I met followed me home.
I climbed yellow heaps of hay

as though they were mountains. maybe
I was a girl from Illinois and I knew it

all along. the city and trains I claimed
as mine. the endless farms, the shopping

malls. but maybe I knew Florida better
than I thought. the blue water there. sun

somehow hotter. in bed, I sleep and I am
underwater. I watch a man jump from

a bridge and he doesn't even scream. I am from
underneath. I dig deeper and piles of dust

rise around me. when I was a girl from
nowhere. when I was a girl. when I was.

Prehistory

I wanted to be an archaeologist
until my mother told me my office

would be in the basement of a museum
and my lungs would fill with dust.

still, I learned the names of dinosaurs
and identified the difference between

a shoulder blade and a pelvis in middle
school science. I dug into the fetal pig's

cold belly while a boy pulled my hair.
I bleached the skull of a mouse that I found

in the woods. I remember when I found a dead
spider perched on its head like a crown. when

I promised my mother I wouldn't dig up bones
for a living, I only meant in deserts and far away

forests. I only meant to not dig up what others
bothered burying. I only meant the bones

that didn't belong to me.

The Field Museum

I remember the bones bigger. I remember
the echo and the pillars.
Sue is skinned and her head is heavy.

in the terracotta warrior exhibit,
the stable boy guards a room
of dead birds. even the horses

in their bone and leather. my father studies
a map and closes his blind eye.
his leather jacket a crown of blood.

my tattoos lifting away from my skin
like fickle monarchs—something
I have disremembered. in the basement,

I am shrunk to the size of a penny.
a mechanical spider shudders and breaks
the neck of an ant. this: disremembered, too.

I pace around the carved-out shells of cicadas.
all of it looking the same and different
and breathless—the Egyptian exhibit and tombs

and the infant mummy and the miniature
dioramas of men putting organs into jars. all
smaller now, all looking like the same dead things.

my father in another leather jacket and me still
small as a penny. the charging lions
by the vending machines, in all their slick bronze,

in all their movement and muscle and tension,
still speared down. still dead. still gone.

Arlington Park

my body tightening against the asphalt. the coins
slung from my hand into the toll basket. the sureness
of some turns, the uncertainty of others.

the speed limit growls underneath me. the trouble is,
I remember the Six Flags across from the highway, but not
the cemetery one mile away. the roller coasters clinking

up metal spines. a crash of rusty beetles. it's the season
in which I try to forget the racetrack. the sting of manure
in the air. the horses sweating as their muscles churn

in front of me. my hand, reaching for the jockey's
small boot. my car darts through traffic and the air
conditioning breaks down. the brakes groan but

work to do their job. this is when I begin to count
my dead relatives because I have never bothered
to take inventory. yes, I have forgiven myself.

for the bets I made on the beasts. for the car falling
apart in sheets of metal. for forgetting where everyone
was buried. the blinders are made of leather

and oil. I am looking straight ahead.

The Mackinac Fox

I saw the fox after I crossed the bridge. a dead bird filled her mouth—a bloody dinner. an argument of feathers. it was, for that second, a comforting violence. a red streak that knew the food chain and its unbreakable bones. how easy the crow died: a simple organization of road and wood and sky. say I outran the rain that day. say the sun set four times, one after the other in a thunder of blue. it's true, driving for hours is a strange chorus with the wind. a pact made between radio static and the trees. at the gas station, I pull an entire butterfly from the grill of my car. just a week ago, my body groaned through a winter. the butterfly's wings came to a grinding halt. the truth is, I am not that strong.

A Man Tells Me How Difficult My Body Is

to look at. to stitch and pull into
all the beautiful shapes he can imagine.

he tells me I am a nest of bees. a dust storm.
a dead owl. taking up so much space

with my skin and limbs. he must be
an enthusiast of the female body. he must

know the tightness of metal on my back.
he breathes near me and says *what a struggle*

your body must be and his words are liquid steel.
slippery as beetles. the bluffs on the north edge

of the town are black and jagged. the walleye
swarm in the deep clear water. this is the biggest

lake. the largest sea of ice. it is an excellent
customer of space. of taking ships and people

and trees and roads and swallowing them whole.
I want to tell the man that no one has touched me

for three years. maybe this is a lie. maybe this is
the struggle he speaks of. maybe he looks at my neck

like Lake Superior looks at boats made of wood
and men. I know I am obvious. I know I am not

small or easy to throw from a dock.
to look at.
                                    imagine
the shapes.
                        a nest of bees. dust storm.
owl. my skin—
an enthusiast.
                            metal.
a beetle,   struggling.
                                    liquid and

                        jagged. a
swarm of   space
and water.

                        swallowed whole.
                        no one.
a lie.   a struggle,
again. my neck,
        obvious.

                imagine   I am not
easy.

A Man in a Bar Takes a Picture of Me

without my permission. it's because I'm reading a book and this,
he decides, is not enough fun. I should, by all intents and purposes,

be having more fun. so he poses for a selfie. his phone cocked
in my direction. I know what he is doing. my knuckles are white.

I hold the book like a slingshot and a rock. this is something new:
I say nothing. I glimpse the picture on the man's phone and in it,

I am staring right into the lens. he is not bothered. he laughs. I glow
in the orange light of the bar. I cannot forget his hand. his thick

fingers and how he just assumed they owned me. this is the lesson:
my body turns to chalk. my skin forgets its smooth dripping shape

like wax. the next day, ice coats my car in a hardness that scrapes my palms.
when I say forget, I really mean I remember every moment about that night.

the cartoon snapshot sound his phone made. the flash he didn't turn off.
my eyes, alive, in a circle of light—above this man's head, like

he was my sun. like I was a moon, orbiting.

I Will Have Forgotten You by Sunday

UFC fighting plays on the TV in the bar—
men with ground up teeth smile through
blood and do backflips from fences.

the referee takes the hand of the winner and raises
it into the dense black of the arena. his arm
is stained red by the gold lights of the ring.

I am the broken bone. I am the shiny yellow
belt around the man's slick waist. I am
the dumb dove flickering in the chain-link cage.

when you give me your name in the bar,
I will have forgotten you before the bell clangs.
before the man's hand bounces from the blue
mat like a T-bone steak.

this is not to say I am forgetful.
this is not to say you are unimportant.
this is to say I am busy fighting and winning
and losing and keeping my teeth in my mouth.

Beast Fables

we are all animals here—
the wily foxes on two legs, eating
at the dinner table. the crying
wolf's tail caught in the mower.

the tiger in your sister's volleyball
jersey becomes a flurry of blood, and here
is proximity. the animal in all
our skins. behind the glass—
in the gutters.

this is a lesson in fake dead
and real dead. in learning
all the lies. six cats mourning
the death of their brother.

you have a tea party in fur
and feathers. this is the storybook:
seeing your body turn to dust
in the glimmer of mirrors.

in his honest twitching face, you
see what the rabbit really wants.
maybe you become the rabbit,
and then here we are again.

brute and human. shaved,
but still, waking up with hair
in our teeth.

II

We all begin as a bundle of bones lost somewhere in a desert, a dismantled skeleton that lies under the sand. It is our work to recover the parts.

—*Clarissa Pinkola Estés*

Wolf Question

she grows thin and howls in search
of something. sixty percent of wolf pups die.

every wild wolf has already survived
a coldness. an empty den and the bodies

of brothers turning to ice. every wolf
mother forced to notice the not-there of her family.

      *

        she can't imagine how it feels,
        to hoard a big painful nothing and hope

        it will live. the girl survives in the woods:
        broken bones and fractures. she survives

        on Isle Royale. fifteen miles inland she shovels
        her car out of her driveway.

Scrape

before I knew love,
I lost thirty-two pieces of me—
a catalog of blood
and quarters.

my jaw had divorced itself.
my teeth spun in
tessellations.

I let my incisors swing,
played them like chimes
over the bathroom sink,

before my father clutched
my chin and clawed
them from my mouth.

this was the first time
a man took something
of mine as his own.

I never learned to keep myself
as myself.

once, my dentist scraped too hard
and a tooth sprung
from my mouth like a penny.
they caged my teeth like clumsy wings.

when I swallowed a tooth,
I dreamt that it was burrowing
inside me—becoming an extension
of bone.

now, I dream that my teeth
crumble away like dry bread,
fall from my mouth like dead birds.

Of Men & Birds

thrust your hook into his pelvis
and suspend him in midair. this
is so you can work with both
hands.

be gentle with his neck. give his legs
a coat of arsenical soap—it protects
him from insects. disjoint his bones

carefully. fill him up. with cotton,
dry leaves, grass, or
crumpled paper. wood wool
is driest and best.

when you take him home,
notice his body: like a great
downy pillow. his bill
as long as a fence rail.

and what wings! and such feet!
you have never seen such a bird,
not even in your dreams.

in your dreams, he is an old,
rusty, second-hand crow. he
is some good genius.

a thimbleful of arsenic. a pair
of eyes black as ink.

when you stitch him up,
make sure to treat him like
a lucky bird, not a greasy swan.

he should have a few stitches
at his back, but not too many.
for obvious reasons.

you wouldn't want him
to look a fool.

Mapping My Father

and the houses he has lived in. the grave
      where his mother is buried. the grave that, someday,

looks like my own. at the green house, my father's ghost
      throws rocks at the brick wall of the storage facility

next door. the train tracks run down the center
      of the street. he places pennies under the wheels

as they burn by in a crash of metal. this home at the end
      of the lake. where the water stops and says *look*.

the truth doesn't always hurt—sometimes the town is
      just the town. the siding is painted green and it breaks

my father's heart. sometimes, the flowers in the cemetery
      and the graves are dead and it doesn't feel like anything.

I forgive all these things. I forgive the broken air
      conditioning, the loneliness that feels round as an egg.

I forgive my father, too. for his discolored smile. all
      the ways he tore me down to bone and built me up

again in blood and light. for catching me when I held

        my breath too long. I wanted that wood floor. that fall.

that wet freshly cut lawn. I need to wake up. I wonder

        where my father will be buried. next to the grave that is

my name. next to his father who has a place. the gulls

        in Michigan City scream like they know all the answers.

they have the keys to every prison in town.

Knives before Forks

my thumb is a dagger
and a spoon—carrying
a clip of apple to my teeth.

my father gives me a set of knives
for my birthday and in this moment,
I am the wooden block—
I am the dark recesses into which
the knife slides deeper.

the handles are heavy and black
and my knuckles fit around them
like round stones slung together
with leather.

when I was young, my bones
were not strong enough to push
through meat. they flexed against
the knives and forks until
the plate chipped into blue.

my father cut the ribeye, red
with blood and gristle,
into manageable tragedies.

my fingers curled around forks
but did not know the name for tongue.

I am still trying to learn
to be wholly metal. to carry
eggs without them tumbling
from the spoon.

For a Moment

I take a picture of a picture
and the photo paper
glares white in the light.
the framed glass—
a fragile layer. a memory.

I am in my father's office,
surrounded by his shiny
synthesizer equipment, waiting
for the printer to work.
its dumb body stutters.

on the desk, a small
silver frame. beveled
edges. slippery velvet
backing. my grandfather
inside—handsome, young.

the side of his suit
jacket tucked behind
his hip, his hand
on his belt. the wind
blowing his tie askew.

the backdrop: a silky blue
curtain. my grandmother
next to him. cat-eye
glasses. gingham
shirt dress.

biting her lip. not dead
at all. I meet her
in this glass box.
we shift
our names around

in our pockets. clumsy
letters mix and
split between us.
they do not know
what is coming. her deep

and bloodless sleep.
his mouth sweet
with smoke. her young
face of milk. his cheeks
like strong hammers.

her earrings, small

circles of moon. I slip

the photo out and

I take a picture, but

each time, they look more

like ghosts. less like my blood.

his grip on her shoulder—

tight and unimaginary.

her tongue on her lips,

holding a word.

Bad Hunter

at the Taxidermy World Championships in Missouri,
women flock around like smart pink birds. they comb

their small foxes with toothbrushes, and preen the wings
of swallows. men wearing leaves chew on toothpicks.

women with sharp bangs and blue glasses pull at the lips
of whitetail deer. one paints the tongue of a rat a sweet

blushy rose. the mounted heads of bucks are lined in neat
rows like an army. the judges wear thin glasses and flash bright

little lights. this is how wet the nose should be, this is how
cocked the hoof. a girl dusts paint flecks off of her roadkill

beaver. a boy licks a pearl of blood from his thumb.

Raw Honey

on the hills of the Antelope Valley Poppy Reserve in California,
the blooms of the state flower billow like small red dresses.

like orange streaks of citrus. the poppies are thin hipped, silky
and hammered with fire. my sister tears the poppies from the ground

like weeds. she hides her heroin in the car we share.
like some kind of milky and boiled down

monster. it's not the same. I know. but the opium poppy looks
just as much like blood. when the poppies die in California, the valley

looks like a great wide grave. like the same slash and burn a world away.
when the opium poppies' petals fall apart like lanterns of fire, the bulb

is cut with a knife. pressed into a brick. strained through burlap and dead
stems of a flower that once was decoration. that once knew nothing

but to bloom.

Stopping Time

if you want to see God, peel back the skin of a
mouse's tail. see the small bones clicking their way

up in steps of pearl. nothing dies that doesn't need
to be dead. nothing is skinned that shouldn't be

turned inside out. when you hold a skull in your hand
it is suddenly more than bone. more than a maze

of holes and structure. when you are elbow deep
in fur, the bird becomes a small piece of emerald,

the beetle a blue opal. a trophy of blood or a recreation
of wind and wings broken back. there is a pot in the kitchen

labeled "for bones only," and it is a metal burnt black.
the skeletons are replaced with wooden dowels and wire.

in this rehydration of skin, you cheat death like it was just
a mess left on stained concrete. but there is your wall,

full of these dry dead things. all preened. all shined.
all waiting. like smart little crowns.

Grasp

I learn the word for willow tree.
I learn the word for howl and keep

it in my throat. the word for wolf
curls underneath my tongue. I have

studied pain this way—tucking it
into the folds of my body where

darkness settles. I wonder about
the waking. the sunsplit

morning burns into orange peel—
dappled heat. an extinct

volcano comes back to life
but we aren't told how we know

the mountain has begun to stir. how
stone yawns and spins hot into

the world again. I wish that I could
say that I saved the mourning dove,

but I can't be sure. every bird dies
a death—falls from the sky and

sleeps. it is hard to banish this thought—
that everything wakes up and waits

for living. for the word that names
the blue color of a pale vein.

who wouldn't want to wake an ancient
thing from the deepest sleep? who

wouldn't want to dig and find the still-wet
blood of a long-dead fawn? a miracle,

maybe, how the earth shudders beneath
us. how we dance along the fractures.

Inventory

let me tell you a secret: I am terrified
of space but in love with the moon.
its pearl circle settles into night. my body—
a flash of poison. pulsing twists & groans.
I carry it over curb & gravel. over
my heavy shame & the sharp dawn.

I am not sure why it scares me—
the up there of the universe.
my unfamiliar musculature.
untied shoes & the dull clunk
of my feet against concrete.
I know the movements, but
they feel unfamiliar.

I concentrate on the moon at 6am.
there is a sick darkness in me.
the small speakers hung on each light post
screech with sounds of grackles.
crackling static recordings. trees empty
and humming.

the wind is where I will it.

this is my inventory:

caged wolf of my heart.

the snarl that carved me out of the sky.

red ache of my mouth.

and what now?

a storm collapses into

my palms. I will never forget it:

how afraid I was.

it is a gathering. a hoard. dew

slicks my ankles. my breath is

the breath of the earth. it growls

and twitches in my chest.

the city melts into

a different shape than it was before.

III

There is a girl inside.
She is randy as a wolf.
—*Lucille Clifton*

Wolf Question

let's remember the hollowness
inside. what once took her blood and grew.

on Isle Royale on Lake Superior, wolves
dance with moose and try to live

through the winter. fifty wolves
slowly becomes two. the wolves die. we forget them.

     *

    and her hands chafe and crack.
    she loses no daughters and loves

    nothing that will hurt or kill
    her. when she moved to the Upper

    Peninsula, she thought there would
    be more wolves. she never sees one.

In Praise of the Exoskeleton

the ability to stay entirely untouched.
unscavenged. unhaunted by the other

bodies inside your own. once, pavement
split me right down the middle. I learned

my blood and its spread. the lengths
my skin went to in its healing. the way I lost

and lost and came back—bright. pink. new.
when men tell me what to think of my body,

I pull my bones around me like a slick jacket
of white. harder this way. rigid and resistant.

ready for rocks. there are mechanics to this
method. to becoming a shell and staying soft

underneath. there's failure, too. in the scales
I develop in direct sunlight. in the cracks

that let the light in. the superglue that won't hold
me. the doctor told me I will never grow taller

and I said, *that's fine*. people always see me
as taller than I am. I am elastic energy.

when you're not looking, I am a swarm of locusts.
when you touch me, it sounds like thunder.

Parenthood

when I see the small bead
of blood on my cat's nose

        I am shocked and I don't know
        why because I know what she

is made of. her blood and
fur and redness and bone.

        but the way her skin
        opened up to claw. the blood

dripping on the carpet. my other
cat snarling from the wingback

        chair. her teeth sharp and
        white and taking over her

sweet face. how the little
animal body puffs up with

        hate, with sound and low
        rumbling noises. my human

skin buckling, too. all that
blood churning underneath.

Extinct

the Eyewitness Book
invertebrates and
the mummified frog.
banded flint. problematica—
in a series of bone. amber
years, I am thankful to be
circumstance of
a man I do not know.
tasted under my tongue.
of a nail. the sweet breath
please, I need you to be
growth and height. the
redwoods and the
gold of an oil slick.
on the beach of a desert.

of fossils and the lost skeleton
spine and the footprint of
the horse tooth.
what cannot be classified
and soft sediment. most
seen. the favorable
disappearance. memory is
not a soft soil I have
today, it is the pounding
of a bat. a hummingbird.
conifer wood. ringlets of
fossilized sequoia and all the
dawn. at once. be the black
be a bone museum
be eating the sun.

Cuffing Season

see "urge," see "how to know if something has bitten you."
wait for the cold to come. wait until your bed is glacial enough

to take the down blanket out of the closet. your friend
laughs and says *it's cuffing season* but she really wants to say:

any love you feel right now isn't love, but a yearning
for warmth. remember what you looked like at twenty-one.

you were so different then. so hopeful. unsure of your shoulders.
you were nothing. you were wanting for winter. for snow.

everything in the before. you left the dead behind and knew it. left
everything to wolves. you believed in no one. you were young.

you had plenty of time. you went west. you let your car run into rust.
you looked back and laughed when the wind called your name.

now, you convince yourself you know this place—you name it an animal.
softness beneath your feet. large empty sounds carved from the air.

the plateau stretches out forever. like metal—dull sheets of gold.
you remember the trees more than anything. the shade. the shadows

they threw across the earth. rocks, wilds, and woods. your body
shoved into fog. between the barn and trees and brooks and birds.

this is the river where your love died. when you burned it, the fire
curled up. your mouth was open and warm. you were so different then.

The Lizard That Lived Forever

I hate to say that I dream about men, but I do. about men who have gone off and married other girls. moved to other colonial houses in Virginia. it is like strapping the tree branch to my bicycle and riding until I become concrete.

*

Monday drew a circle around me and lit it on fire. Wednesday learned my name and spit it onto my lap.

*

I scrub an opal earring with a wire brush and it turns to gold in my hands. I have dug it out of a dead woman's pink jewelry box. I was born in October, and I feel like I need to polish all of the opals that ever existed.

*

this morning, a man walks into the store where I work and tells me he is an ordained minister. he asks to see an antique straight razor and cradles the carved handle in his hands like a small bird.

*

the truth is, my sister will not feed the pet lizard so the crickets jump around our house like small flickers of light. they sing to each other. the lizard jumps from our palms as though she has never been afraid. when she dies, she curls under a rock and turns to dust. we bury her in the backyard as though we loved her.

*

when the man at the store tells me what he thinks of my body, I want to tell him that I haven't been touched in three years. maybe I am lying. maybe this is the struggle he speaks of.

*

I think about my sister's lizard. how we named her a name I don't remember. I think about how she lived longer than all the other lizards. I think about the strange scars left behind on my body—their pale and vicious takeover. the part I do remember: applying medicine every night, peeling off the scab in the morning, and doing it all over again. and again.

*

I see the man again. and this time, I shrink into a hummingbird. I try to laugh at his jokes and show my teeth. what he doesn't know is that I feel all the poison. I smell it on his skin. on his scabby arms. his combat boots are laced tight and tall as though they have never left his feet.

*

maybe a stranger is someone I have never met. maybe he takes a picture of me without my permission. maybe he is five beers deep and reeks of smoke. maybe a stranger owns my body, in some sick and unfair way. he knows what will make me move down the bar. he knows what will make me shift in my seat until my dress becomes a chrysalis.

*

this is to say: I have never forgiven myself for the times I smiled when I should have screamed. for the men who asked when they knew the answer. the last time I saw you, I ran through the parking lot like a deer caught in the line of fire. of course, I could just take the blindfold off. of course, I could just let you shoot me and it'd all be over.

*

before the overgrown lawn. before the man. before all the men. before I buried my trust in the sea. before I ate a fig for the first time and it felt like a universe found its way into my mouth. I never knew survival like that. how to say thank you but with needles in your teeth.

*

in the end—all dust. the lizard. the rusty razorblade. we have all known too many cheeks. we have all known too many men who will tell us what they think without caring at all.

*

I will never forget what you said to me when you left: you begged me to stop speaking. you begged me to stop saying your name.

Renovation

this time, we say *rally, rally win.* we condition the leather

until supple. we talk about the men we have lost as if

they had never been anything but lucky to touch us. it's like

this: the orange peels gone limp in the yard. the glasses, old

and sticky in the sink. the wallpaper peeling like a snake. good

grief, the guns in the closet are dusty and bulletless. good grief,

the inside is made of oil and liquor. when the chalkboard

turns into a dark swarm of wasps, I have forgotten how my name

denies my body like water and butter. the beads of yellow lifting

to the surface like small stubborn suns.

Lamb without a Mother

when my mother's water broke in the hotel room,
I clung to the warmth inside. the doctor pulled me

by my shoulders until my collarbone snapped. until
I broke out of my mother in a messy splinter of bone.

in the artificial womb, the pink lamb shudders. the womb
is named Eve. let's name the lamb "breath" or "baby"—

her hooves already sharp and black. her eyes closed.
moving beneath the lids. her ears flickering in the fluid.

the plastic bag around her bony knees.
a grip of viscous liquid. the life kept inside. a clear

tube feeds the lamb fetus bright red blood. like a mother.
like an umbilical cord. the lamb is alive. the lamb is being born.

the lamb isn't broken. at all.

Rifle Season

they come north for the woods.
for the soggy overhang of trees.

the dampened noise and the echo.
for the deer. the blood. the bullets.

quick and vicious. the season brings
the deer blinds. men become the forest.

they rock their guns to sleep, cradle
the metal bodies. here for the fur

harvesting. the trapping. the hard
and silver teeth. the stocked freezers

swirling with ice. with ink-dark meat,
sinew. blood unravels onto concrete

floors in damp garages. these men do not
surprise me—their hands dirty, coarse.

their tongues turn to gold in their mouths.
they apologize, but their teeth are steel

cages. they chomp and glint—they sparkle.
it doesn't matter— I'm wounded. I limp

into a clearing lit by the sun. maybe I'll be safe here.
I'm always surprised when they find me.

the men: more and more of them tumble
from the fog. their breath dirties the melting

snow. the deer, even, spooked. hooves hurried
and sharp. maybe I'll wear fluorescent orange

next time. maybe I'll carry a whistle that calls the sky.
the grouse, the crow, a camouflage of birds.

Woolly Bones

you get one day to dig, the farmer said, *the harvest is here.*
this could have been the cornfield on the corner where the white
dog barked at cars. this could have been my sister's cigarette
hiding spot—in the skull of the beast.

there's a mammoth in Michigan. there's tusks in my backyard.
there's vertebrae in my teeth. this could have been
the mud in my basement.

once, a deer left its head in a hayfield off the road.
with a shovel, I hid it in the trees.
I polished its ribs with bleach. this was a death I knew.

maybe the mammoth was hungry, or cold, or ancient, or sick,
or so sure it was dying and the raw field of green seemed
like the right sleep, seemed like the right spot to fertilize
the crop—but maybe killed by spear or arrow.
kept in a pond as a prize. the bones showed signs of butchering.

those soybeans must have burst from the ground the year they planted.
I wonder if the farmer questioned that first grassy crop. doubted
how the corn was sweetest the next year. knew how mud ran
so deep it hit bones, how water pooled there in the heavy season.

noticed how the rain knew where the thirst was, or how sometimes,

when he tilled the fields, the dirt flew through the air

like fur.

Blossom Rot

you may wonder what I'm doing here—
planting lilies in
your backyard, elbow deep
in earth. see, I have dug up
these worms for you:
pink ribbons for your hair.

this is how I tell you I love you.
from the dirt-sweet wet of my mouth,
I give you two acorns.

crows assemble
on the long necks of pines,
a dog whimpers on my walk home,
tied to a white porch.
a man and woman drag metal detectors
through their tangled yard.

this is how I tell you I love you.
love, as in, you bury me.

I give you antler velvet,

a pinecone the size of a fox,

I give you a lightning bolt,

I give, and the giving

is a shadow of bats.

in the yawn of the hangnail

moon, I eat my own wings.

I am too tired for the heavy door.

I give you

a handful of gutted lilies

and name them my heart.

Fever

I have some explaining to do—
the gun wasn't mine. I didn't lose the keys

but knew I'd never need them again.
I twisted them in the door until the metal

broke into silver. until the lock had
swallowed them up. the bullets were really

unburied roses. the bulbs still fleshy and soft—
dormant in the winter. the truth is, I often

think of the routes we ran. the bristle
of our furs. the way we punched down

hunger and ice and made them obey.
when a baby screams, it all floods back—

the unflinching stumps of dead trees. the way
I cry back at the face of something wailing.

my body calling out and me, smothering
it into silence. into awkward and hungry

submission. the wolves make the thunder
in the night. I can hear them. they make

my blood run warm.

Mud Ceremony

today, the jackal marries
the fox. the fox is dead
but still red as a split lip—
a clumsy pair.

the jackal is a witch kissing
her wife—the sunshower
wets her fur like a compulsion
of storm, of sun beat to blue
fire. a bright devil.

there are many things I have never done.
buy a lottery ticket. call
a radio station. play slots.
catch a bouquet of wisteria
or rats. a plague. maybe

I'm the witch—the wolf
in a wedding dress. I can't
say why the crow I marry
isn't in the folklore—
isn't in the black book.

when the rain spills from
the sky's mouth like milk—
somewhere, a wife is crying.
maybe I'm the wife. the devil
beating me, fighting
over my chicken bone,

bloody, stripped of meat.
this is when the funfair
begins. when the weather
turns salty—whips the dead
fox redder.

IV

The truth is we know little about the wolf. What we know a good deal more about is what we imagine the wolf to be.

—*Barry Lopez*

Wolf Question

fifteen miles inland something else
happens. a girl learns how best

to survive. the wolves: everywhere,
running across the ice, chasing food

and blood and love. still, they continue
to live and die and starve and live.

*

she sees a red fox, maybe, a yellow sign signaling
a moose crossing. they're there, she knows.

deep in the Hiawatha forest. when she
Googles "wolf howl" a frequently

asked question appears: "what sound
does a wolf make when it is happy?"

Call Me a Courage

I want to name all the birds. to identify kingdom and phylum and order. a taxonomy
of beaked jaws. hard shells. feathers—I forget, sometimes, that we name everything

that bleeds. I want to categorize their clumsy syllables. know them by their candy-

colored wings. the soft nakedness of their feet. I want to call out to them—
each one, by its name, as though I had known it all along. in the museum diorama,

their bodies are mid-flight. perched. diving into glass. oh, those four-chambered hearts.

the hollow bones of flightless deaths. funny how we strive to name
a prowl of jaguars. a streak of tigers. how we name companionship as though

it is something surprising to want. to need. a brash of deer lingers in the dew-wet

lawn of my childhood home. chewing clover. blinking into the dense fog. I wonder:
what would we name a group of me? twenty versions of my body shift in a field.

my skin collects wetness at dawn. I'm skittish, maybe. I look for shelter. a dissimulation

of birds watches from the tree line. a host of sparrows bursts from an oak in a splash
of darkness. black-throated. everyone looks beautiful in white. like doves—feathered

romantic things. on my side of the glass, the creatures I see are always more frightening.

let's name us a murder. a courage. a loneliness.

The Girl Who Cried Wolf

in the hospital room, my pregnant mother breathes
in sharp shaking bursts. my father is wearing a tux.

I have never seen him in a bow tie. his hair looks soft
& I reach to touch it but come back with air. Chicago's

sweet breath. my mother's gown sticks to her neck & I can
hear my body entering the world. she is a salt-licked ocean.

my father is crying & laughing & grinding his teeth. I have
never known my parents as liars, but I am sure they have lied

many times. about many things. where my teeth went as I placed
them under my pillows in handfuls. what happened to the squirrel

trapped in our attic. his little fragile body. in the hospital room
I think to call out, but my voice is the creaking of the door.

the blip of my mother's heart monitor. & there I am, crying
& red & already learning to lie. I reach for the blanket

I am swaddled in. my hand comes back with a fistful of ash.
I have touched the lies & they want me back.

Little Griefs

we have never met, but we were in the same place at the same time. now, the stained-glass window creates a madness of light. blades of sun slice through the snowshine—April in an icy dress. a small panther crawls out of the sea. a girl becomes a statue made of cement and wood and metal. this is how grief arrives—like a slow groan coaxed from an axe. its steel buried in a tree. in the black hole spring, a lake glows in the dark and we traverse it, spin across it like bark. like honey coated on our tongues. name this place: the blue sky opening its mouth. these must be our ghosts— they're all over us. they're escaping out of our skins.

Favor

after Li-Young Lee

a field of poppies blooms
between my fingers—
my father grabs a needle
and tells me to hold still.

I am not a patient child,
or a curator of pain, so I become
a young bird,
underneath.

I dig at a splinter
until my palm begins to bleed.
a rose opens.

I remember my small white hand,
a ceramic plate, and a circle
of red, growing as the heart
in my palm pulsed free.

my father's voice is low,
and his fingers are much bigger
than mine—he loses me
in a story about Lake Shore Drive,
or fire, or paddling a boat.

the wood is released from me,
and I don't
cry, but place my mouth
over the cut—feeling
foreign, feeling like the hand
of a bird.

I am not patient. my father
whispers in a clatter of silver.
I become an eagle,
underneath—
my father, preening my wings.

Shear

this is a place of joy, I guess. the sun rises and sets
in brassy exclamations of light. I write poems

about being in love with nobody but wind.
my mouth is a little red animal. I love lightning—

I live at the top of a hill and roll my body down
until my bones hit lake. it is a big fake dream, living

here in a house made of ghosts. it is easy
to be invisible in the woods. if I start making

a movie out of my life. if I pan out to show
a blue car rumbling through Kentucky. if I cut open

the chest of a wolf and find milk. what then?
I could leave here forever and never come back.

I'll say: this is the road I traveled away from
this place. this is the national forest that cried

out my name as I drove. this is the coyote I saw
as I left the state. I've never seen a coyote, but

I sometimes dream of heaven. every place I have
known has hurt me. this is to say

that I miss the soft things. feeling safe
in crosswalks of cities I love. I drop a pair

of scissors and catch them, the shears
open against my hand like wings.

Glass Gravity

I didn't ask you to open your mouth like that   I didn't ask

for your body to turn towards me like a sundial   your eyes small

and ticking clocks   I haven't thought about that penny I found

on the ground for weeks   it has been sitting in my pocket

going unspent   cast in bronze

in this scene, I am in love or asleep all summer   naked

waiting for any butcher to have at my body   in its steam and sweat and salt

its rich and unthankful blood   I often see my face in the slick

of gasoline on the road   in the concrete

birdbath split down the middle

what delicious gravity   what a waste to have never

felt clean

This Is the Realm of Last Chances

this could be anything: airplanes, mice, socks, wolves. these sounds, they turn to ghosts in the night. their howls become me. somehow, I always find a way to write about birds, even when I know that everyone expects me to write about birds. their wings, maybe. their small and yellow beaks. their flight and descent and the patterns they make in the sky. there I go, my obsession turning to ash. I will give you all the wolf poems and call them a pack, a family, a hunt. I will pretend I know danger and its definitions. there is a place for all of this, some last chance that erases fear. that wraps up my vague and bloom-red scars into lush bouquets of blood. this is how I search for wolves. find my blindness in a place I cannot name. it is a weakness, coming to the woods and forgiving the shore. I cannot own or disown anything. not in the right way. everything—too final for its own good.

Origin of the Mapping System

I was potentially everything. a glass atlas—
my legend bled dry with the clean cut

of a knife. no: I have never scorched my body
in search of warmth. I bury myself in sand

and it is everything I expect. I am filled: I find
the grains later, and they are small planets

I have taken and kept. polished slivers
of quartz. my skin is a scavenger hunt. a map

of where pain bloomed around me like milk.
where I studied how my bones clicked. snapped.

I loved a man. he made me a girl
who listened well. all I wanted was the good

and beautiful things I had heard about. and who
could blame me. I wanted pleasure. to be

touched in wet terrestrial places. I wanted
to loosen into bright shards of earth.

once, I pretended that I wore a crown

of opals. of the richest dirt-sweet soil.

Circumstances of Disappearance

it is easy enough to say it: I want
                    to be an orange
harvest moon. cantaloupe sky. people
                    driving into the dark
country just to see. bitten

                    by mosquitos. burrs
clinging to milky ankles.
                    that dappled moon
that the wolf looks at and speaks to.
                    the craters and cliffs. pains-

taking detail. every wrinkle
                    on my face. I am not
sure when I stopped believing
                    that I was beautiful, but I did
& there is no going back.

                    I want & the wanting
just becomes easier. my body
                    swallows it up until my bones howl
like wolves. I want to be a puddle
                    with a world living inside.

slick that never dries up,

        pooling in the craters

of uneven parking lots. forever

        wet & weeping things.

I want to be the small sliver

        of metal in my mother's finger.

the scorched wall

        of my father's aortic valve.

I want to be blood—

        its intricate deliberate maze.

I want to be a planet &

        a canyon. splinter & a tear

in the sky. I will admit it:

        sometimes I just want

to hear my name out loud.

Look What I Have Done

I welcomed you like a hood of antlers.

like bone broke down to velvet. like growth
and the wind that raised me. in my mind,

heaven is full of animals the earth didn't get to keep.

nice things taken away from a shrieking child
with red cheeks. the dodo. the Tasmanian tiger.

the hartebeest. the passenger pigeon. inside me:

some goddess of war. maybe she carries a bow
and arrow. maybe she is sculpted of marble.

it is Friday, and I am swallowing the sun.

the rats in my parent's backyard are so big, so strong,
that they take the traps with them. they snap

in the night, but the yard is empty. my womanhood

hibernates in the winter. blows shrill whistles in the damp
mornings. croons the dead birds into small funerals

of feathers. I must stay calm so as to preserve my wings.

you could destroy them easily, just like that.
with the bark of a tree. with a small gun.

My Father Asks If I Was Raised by a Jackal

he laughs but he knows what he did. he molded my blood.

    I became part wolf while driving

        the lawnmower. my nails sharpened into blades.

    I remember the day I woke up

with hair in my throat. I ran twenty miles in the snow

    and didn't get tired. I shaved my legs but the fur

        kept growing back. my palms turned rough

    and thick with grit. my father threw me down

the stairs but I landed on all fours. I ate my steaks

    with less and less salt. more blood—no knives.

        my sister and mother kept their distance.

    they cleaned up the messes I'd make. my father

groomed the wolf in me—threw slices of meat at me

    in the yard, live rabbits, flightless baby birds.

        he kept me outside in the winter, to see

    how long I would last, how hot my heart

would pump. once all my teeth fell out, I knew

    I couldn't go back. in their place, long silvery fangs.

        sharp bones cutting my lips. I blinded my mother

    when I kissed her goodnight. I ran away the next day.

I killed small animals in the woods nearby. I kept warm

    in the rotting leaves, the mud. sometimes, at night,

        I could hear my father. he was howling for me.

    at the moon. at the ink-black of the sky.

Alpha

I am good at being a wolf.
I am good at being a lamb.
I am one thing
and I am another.

this is what my hands are for:
a sharp knife, slippery metal,
dark blood, cleaning
my fur, peeling a plum.

it is crucial that I survive—
that I lead the pack and live.
I can't keep my wolf teeth
hidden.

Bramble and Knife

never mind the string of lights that died before all the others.
never mind the last white wolf in Yellowstone limping, red,

through the dense night. no one can ever tell me this is fate,
how everything goes about dying like it does. how the goat's eyes

flicker in sweet quadrilaterals before the knife chomps its teeth
metallic. when a boy jumps from a bridge in my hometown, his face

looks like my young grandfather, or my never-born brother. my sister
skips another funeral of a friend gone missing. she polishes

the glasses in her sink until her skin glares red. listen: I am drawing
diagrams of the frostbitten grass. of the small untouched bodies

of birds. in some other life, I am breathing, and my heart does not
skip in my throat like a river-worn stone.

Acknowledgements

Grateful acknowledgement is given to the editors of the following publications in which the following pieces, sometimes in earlier versions, first appeared:

Split Rock Review: "Self-Portrait as Mammal"
Hunger Mountain: "I Thought There Would Be More Wolves"
Prairie Schooner: "Your Daughter Is a Liar"
Poetry Northwest: "Nesting Material"
Gordon Square Review: "Prehistory"
Tinderbox Poetry Journal: "A Man Tells Me How Difficult My Body Is"
The Rumpus: "A Man in a Bar Takes a Picture of Me", "Rifle Season"
Fairy Tale Review: "I Will Have Forgotten You by Sunday", "Bad Hunter"
Gulf Stream Literary Magazine: "Beast Fables"
Reservoir Journal: "Scrape", "Blossom Rot"
Blueshift Journal (now defunct): "Of Men & Birds"
New South: "Knives before Forks"
Sequestrum: "For a Moment"
TIMBER: "Raw Honey"
Third Coast: "Stopping Time"
Thrush Poetry Journal: "Grasp"
Booth: "In Praise of the Exoskeleton"
CutBank: "The Lizard That Lived Forever"
Third Point Press: "Renovation"
Storm Cellar: "Woolly Bones"
The Molotov Cocktail: "Mud Ceremony"
DIALOGIST: "Call Me a Courage"
The Boiler Journal: "Favor"
Wildness: "Shear" (as "Loving with Scissors")
Hot Metal Bridge: "This Is the Realm of Last Chances"
Kenyon Review: "Origin of the Mapping System"
New Ohio Review: "Circumstances of Disappearance"
Anomaly: "Look What I Have Done"
Sweet: "My Father Asks If I Was Raised by a Jackal"
Sonora Review: "Bramble and Knife"

Some of these poems have also appeared (in earlier versions) in the chapbook *Never Leave the Foot of an Animal Unskinned,* published by Porkbelly Press.

"Grasp" was featured online on *Poetry Daily.*

"Look What I Have Done" was a Web Weekly Feature on *Verse Daily.*

"The Lizard that Lived Forever" was chosen by Andrew Martin as the winner of the 2018 Big Sky, Small Prose Flash Contest at *CutBank.*

Thank you to Elizabeth Bradfield and *Permafrost* for choosing my book, and to University of Alaska Press for publishing it. I hope we meet up North someday.

Immense gratitude to my MFA classmates and professors at Northern Michigan University, especially Austin Hummell, who saw these poems in their rawest forms, Rachel May, who supported and challenged me throughout my time in the program, and Caroline Krzakowski, for her critical eye. Much appreciation to the Excellence in Education Research Program and the Future Faculty Fellowship at NMU, both of which allowed me the time and space to write, teach, and explore the land I love so much. The sharp chill of the Upper Peninsula still lives deep within me. I'll come back to find the wolves.

Thank you to those who welcomed me to the Llano Estacado and Texas Tech University. Thank you to the invaluable advice from Curtis Bauer on the order of these poems, and to Hali, Jacob, Brook, Jess, Kristina, Chloe, Meghan, and the many others who make living in Lubbock easier. You all make me a better person, writer, and scholar.

Thank you to the J.T. and Margaret Talkington Graduate Fellowship and the William Bryan Gates Graduate Award for the generous funding that allows me to focus on my writing. Thank you to Sundress Academy for the Arts at Firefly Farms for giving me a week to write and revise and reflect in the woods; it was a solace, even as it felt like the world was crumbling around us.

I am indebted to my earliest mentors, Jeff Kass and Maureen Seaton, who both sparked and fueled my love for poetry.

Particular thanks to Sarah Bates, Jenna Quartararo, Krys Malcolm Belc, and Natasha Mijares, who have written with me in many coffee shops and bolstered my writing and poetry in more ways than I can count. You are true and forever friends.

Most importantly, infinite thanks and love to my parents, Sharon and Anthony Ryan, for their constant support and kindness along this often-difficult path as an academic and writer. And to my sister, Emily—I am so glad that you are alive and here to read this book. You're my best friend and I love you. This book is for you.

Sara Ryan is the author of the chapbooks *Never Leave the Foot of an Animal Unskinned* (Porkbelly Press) and *Excellent Evidence of Human Activity* (The Cupboard Pamphlet). In 2018, she won Grist's Pro Forma Contest and Cutbank's Big Sky, Small Prose Contest. Her work has been published in *Brevity, Kenyon Review, Pleiades, DIAGRAM, Prairie Schooner, Thrush Poetry Journal* and other journals. She is a managing editor for *Iron Horse Literary Review*. She received her MFA from Northern Michigan University, and is currently pursuing her PhD at Texas Tech University.